WHEN THE FIRE FELL

BY

GEORGE T. B. DAVIS

Author of

"Fulfilled Prophecies That Prove the Bible"
"Rebuilding Palestine According to Prophecy"
"Seeing Prophecy Fulfilled in Palestine"
"Adventures in Soul-Winning"
"Jewels for Messiah's Crown"

Revised Edition

Published and sold by

THE MILLION TESTAMENTS CAMPAIGNS

1505 Race Street, Philadelphia 2, Pa.

DAVID BRAINERD
Indians "came streaming in upon him from all sides, and
grasping the bridle of his horse, besought him to tell them
the way of salvation."

CONTENTS

CHAPTER I

WHEN THE FIRE FELL
FROM HEAVEN

On rare and memorable occasions, in Old Testament times, the fire fell from heaven.

One of these significant events occurred in the life of David. King David had sinned in numbering the people, and judgment was being poured out upon Israel. David earnestly confessed his sin and prayed. God heard his prayer. Judgment was stayed. Then, in obedience to God's command, David built an altar and offered sacrifices. And God "answered him from heaven by fire upon the altar of burnt offering" (I Chronicles 21:26).

Again the fire fell from heaven when Solomon dedicated the Temple. The falling fire signified the divine acceptance of the confession and prayer of his servant Solomon: "Now when Solomon had made an end of praying, the fire came down from heaven, and consumed the burnt offering and the sacrifices; and the glory of the LORD filled the house."

At this marvelous manifestation of God's

power the assembled multitude of the children
of Israel bowed themselves in worship: "And
when all the children of Israel saw how the fire
came down, and the glory of the LORD upon
the house, they bowed themselves with their
faces to the ground upon the pavement, and
worshipped, and praised the LORD, saying, For
he is good; for his mercy endureth for ever"
(II Chronicles 7:3).

Later, Israel departed from the LORD in
following Baal and worshipping idols. The
prophet Elijah called the prophets of Baal and
the children of Israel to Mount Carmel in a
contest to let it be known which was the true
God. Elijah said: "The God that answereth by
fire, let him be God." The prophets of Baal
built an altar and laid a bullock for sacrifice
upon it. All day long they called upon their
god, but there was no response.

At the time of the evening sacrifice Elijah
repaired the altar of the LORD, and laid the
bullock for the sacrifice upon it. At the command of the prophet they filled twelve barrels
with water and poured them upon the sacrifice,
until the water filled the trench about the altar.
Elijah then quietly called upon God to manifest His power in order to bring the people
back to Him: "Then the fire of the LORD fell,

and consumed the burnt sacrifice and the wood, and the stones, and the dust, and licked up the water that was in the trench. And when all the people saw it, they fell on their faces: and they said, The LORD, he is the God; the LORD, he is the God." (I Kings 18:38, 39.)

In New Testament times the "sound of a rushing mighty wind," and "cloven tongues like as of fire" marked the descent of the Holy Ghost on the "birthday" of the Christian Church. This occurred after 120 faithful disciples had spent ten days, between Christ's ascension and the day of Pentecost, "with one accord in prayer and supplication."

Then the "cloven tongues" appeared, and they were all filled with the Holy Ghost. They became flaming witnesses for Christ. Former cowards were transformed into men of boldness and courage. In one day 3000 souls were born again; and on another day, a little later, 5000 souls were saved.

Throughout the centuries since that memorable day of Pentecost God has sent the "fire from heaven" again and again to revive his children, and to lead multitudes of precious souls into the light of the gospel. These heaven-sent visitations of the Spirit have been like enkindling flames—warming, reviving, convicting, converting, empowering, men and women.

This little book is a record of some of these thrilling, never-to-be-forgotten times of revival. May the recounting of these times of blessing encourage us to believe that once again God is waiting to visit his Church with a new outpouring of the Holy Spirit in mighty quickening power! May He make us willing to fulfill the conditions of prayer, confession, and dedication, in order that the fire may fall again upon ourselves and upon our land!

Again and again throughout the centuries of the Christian era, the fire of God has fallen from heaven with untold blessing. In Scotland, in the year 1630, a young minister named John Livingston was invited to preach to a great assembly of people in the open air. Realizing the importance of the meeting, groups of earnest Christians formed themselves into little companies and spent the night in earnest supplication for God's blessing upon the gathering. The young minister himself, John Livingston, was a member of one of the companies of all-night intercessors.

The next day as the hour of the meeting drew near, the young man felt himself utterly unworthy to preach to such a great gathering of people. He felt himself so insufficient for the task that he was preparing to steal away into the fields. However, his friends gathered about him and constrained him to remain. As the young man spoke, the Spirit of God came upon him in great power. His text was Ezekiel 36:25, 26: "Then will I sprinkle clean water upon you, and ye shall be clean. A new heart also will I give you, and a new spirit will I put within you."

For two hours and a half the young man spoke with burning lips to the great audience. The heavenly "fire" fell upon the multitude and the scene was like another Pentecost. Rev. John Shearer in his book "Old Time Revivals" tells the story of what happened:

"The Spirit filled the speaker with a fulness that must be outpoured. The people seemed rooted to the ground in a great stillness. Five hundred men and women, some from the high ranks of society, some poor wastrels and beggars, were converted where they stood, and lived from that day as those who had indeed received a new heart and a new spirit. The memory of that day has never died, and the very telling of the story has proved a fount of revival."

In the early days of the American colonies, the fire of God again fell from heaven in a great spiritual awakening, under the leadership of Jonathan Edwards. During the early part of Jonathan Edwards' ministry in New England we are told that "there was a marked decline in the religious life of the community. Among the young people the bands of morality had sadly relaxed. Frolics continued far into the night, and became the handmaid of vice."

With such conditions about him Jonathan Edwards gave himself to prayer and the ministry of the Word for eight years. Then suddenly the fire fell. Mr. Shearer gives a graphic picture of the scenes that were witnessed as the Spirit of God came down upon the people of the whole community. Suddenly, "conversions began to take place throughout the town. One of the first was that of a frivolous young woman, a leader in the 'frolics.' She became in very truth 'a new creature' so humble, pure, and gracious, so utterly transformed, that she was an object of wonder and amazement. The news of this conversion 'acted like a flash of lightning upon the hearts of the young people'; and as it flew from lip to lip the convicting Spirit seemed to pierce every heart that heard it. Indeed, throughout this revival, probably the most potent awakening agency was the simple news of another's conversion. A hunger for the same blessing was at once aroused in the hearer's heart.

"In the early months of 1735 the people pressed into the church daily, and for a time Northampton was literally filled with the presence of God. In almost every house parents were rejoicing over their children, and in the sanctuary the tears of penitence, of new-found joy, and deep compassion flowed freely. The whole congregation became like a heavenly choir, and praise was a sweet and holy sacrifice.

"The Bible was a new book. Texts that had been read a thousand times appeared with such fresh and novel interest that even old saints were tempted to think they had never seen them before, and regarded them with a strange wonder. Young converts read their Bibles with such eager intensity that their eyes became dimmed and they could not distinguish the letters. The tavern was emptied, and in the streets men paused to speak to one another of the beauty and matchless love of Christ.

"Ministers from other parts came to witness these wonders of Divine Grace. When they recounted them to their people, the Spirit used their testimony, often in a remarkable way.

The fire spread thus from town to town and from county to county. It spread not only throughout New England; it passed also to other lands."

About the time of the awakening in New England there was a remarkable revival among the American Indians, under the leadership of David Brainerd, the apostle to the Indians. It was one of the notable spiritual awakenings in the history of the Christian Church. When Brainerd first began his work among the Indians, he had little success. His health became impaired. He retired from the work for a time. He was offered a pastorate among "wealthy and kindly people," and his heart went out in love toward the daughter of Jonathan Edwards. But day by day he heard in his soul the pitiful cries of the poor lost Indians who were so degraded and steeped in sin.

He made the great decision. He deliberately gave up a life of ease and comfort, and went back into the wilderness to proclaim the gospel to "his poor Indians." With dauntless heroism he went from place to place preaching to various Indian tribes. His tours among the tribes covered "more than three thousand miles, through forests, over dangerous mountains, in fierce rains, and freezing cold."

As time went on Brainerd realized more and more that it was only through the mighty power of God, and the fire falling from heaven, that the hardened hearts of the stolid Indians could be changed. He decided to give himself unreservedly to intercessory prayer. It is said that "whole nights were spent in agonizing prayer in the dark woods, his clothes drenched with the sweat of his travail." As the result of such intense fervent intercession it is little wonder that the windows of heaven were opened and the fire fell. Mr. Shearer tells the thrilling story:

"Suddenly, the Spirit was outpoured upon the whole region of the Susquehanna. His first audience there had consisted of four women and a few children. Now there came streaming in upon him from all sides a host of men and women, who pressed upon him, and grasping the bridle of his horse, besought him with intense earnestness to tell them the way of salvation. In a great, glad wonder he looked upon them, and the text that leaped to his lips was, 'Herein is love.'

"Men fell at his feet in anguish of soul. These were men who could bear the most acute torture without flinching. But God's arrow had now pierced them; their pain could not be concealed and they cried out in their distress, 'Have mercy upon me.' What impressed Brainerd most deeply was that though these people came to him in a multitude, each one was mourning apart. The prophecy of Zechariah was fulfilled before his eyes. The woods were filled with the sound of a great mourning, and beneath the Cross every man fell as if he and the Saviour God alone were there. Gradually as the missionary spoke, there came to them, one by one, the peace and comfort of the Gospel.

"As the days passed he had full proof that a heaven-sent revival had come. A passion for righteousness possessed the converts. The wretched victims of the 'fire-water' were delivered, and the Indian camps were cleansed at once from their physical and moral filthiness. The love of Christ expelled every unlovely thing. As one poor woman expressed it, 'Me to be Him for all,' became the motto of their lives. They became themselves ardent missionaries of the Cross. The light spread through all that dark region, and a strong Indian Church was established."

In another land across the sea the fire fell from heaven in answer to earnest intercessory

prayer. In the early part of the eighteenth
century the spiritual life of the people of
Great Britain was at a low ebb. Moral and
spiritual declension was much the same as in
America and Great Britain at the present
time.

But John Wesley and George Whitefield
and others of like mind, were not content to
let conditions remain in a state of stagnation.
They were men of vision, men of faith, men of
prayer. They began to cry to God for an
outpouring of His Spirit. Whole nights were
spent in intercessory prayer. At length the
fire of God fell upon them in the early morning hours of one of these all-night prayer
meetings. Wesley in his Journal tells what
happened: "About three in the morning, as we
were continuing instant in prayer, the power
of God came mightily upon us, insomuch that
many cried out for exceeding joy, and many
fell to the ground."

Filled with the Spirit of God, Wesley and
Whitefield and others went everywhere
preaching the gospel. Like a gale from heaven
they went up and down the British Isles
preaching to vast multitudes sometimes numbering 20,000 and more. Their zeal for souls
was so great that they came over to America

and helped greatly in evangelizing our new land. The Rt. Hon. Lloyd George, British Prime Minister during the first world war, declared that the revival under Wesley changed the history of the British Isles.

CHAPTER II

WHEN THE FIRE FELL AGAIN IN AMERICA

One of the most remarkable revivals in the history of the Christian Church was that which swept over the United States in the middle of the nineteenth century. It was born in prayer, and carried forward through earnest intercessory prayer throughout the nation. The great awakening was known as the "Revival of '57."

The revival meetings conducted by Charles G. Finney before the great awakening of '57 were doubtless the fount and mainspring of that amazing work of grace. Mr. Finney was filled with the Spirit of God and for some two-score years went up and down the United States like a gale from heaven.

Mr. Finney was a lawyer in the State of New York. Much prayer ascended to the Throne for his conversion. Finally he was saved and received a mighty infilling of the Holy Spirit at the time of his conversion. This remarkable outpouring of the Spirit of God upon the young lawyer was doubtless God's call to him to become an evangelist, and to preach the gospel with such power as few men have proclaimed it since the days of the apostle Paul.

Mr. Finney, in his autobiography, tells the story of how the Spirit of God came upon him in mighty power. Let me give the narrative in Mr. Finney's own words:

"I rushed into the room back of the front office, to pray. There was no fire, and no light, in the room; nevertheless it appeared to me as if it were perfectly light. As I went in and shut the door after me, it seemed as if I met the Lord Jesus Christ face to face. It seemed to me that I saw him as I would see any other man. He said nothing, but looked at me in such a manner as to break me right down at his feet. It seemed to me a reality, that he stood before me, and I fell down at his feet and poured out my soul to him. I wept aloud like a child, and made such confessions as I could with my choked utterance. It seemed to me that I bathed his feet with my tears; and yet I had no distinct impression that I touched him.

"As I turned and was about to take a seat by the fire, I received a mighty baptism of the

Holy Ghost. Without any expectation of it, without ever having the thought in my mind that there was any such thing for me, without any recollection that I had ever heard the thing mentioned by any person in the world, the Holy Spirit descended upon me in a manner that seemed to go through me, body and soul. I could feel the impression, like a wave of electricity, going through and through me. Indeed it seemed to come in waves and waves of liquid love; for I could not express it in any other way. It seemed like the very breath of God. I can recollect distinctly that it seemed to fan me, like immense wings.

"No words can express the wonderful love that was shed abroad in my heart. I wept aloud with joy and love; and I do not know but I should say, I literally bellowed out the unutterable gushings of my heart. These waves came over me, and over me, and over me, one after the other, until I recollect I cried out, 'I shall die if these waves continue to pass over me.' I said, 'Lord, I cannot bear any more'; yet I had no fear of death."

Mr. Finney began his ministry in the towns and villages in the district where he was living. Then, filled with the Spirit of God, he went on to an everwidening evangelistic ministry both in the United States and in the British Isles.

One of the most remarkable experiences of Mr. Finney's evangelistic work occurred in a district in New York that was so ungodly that it was nicknamed "Sodom." There was only one godly man in the place and they called him "Lot." This man invited Mr. Finney to preach in a school house in the community but said nothing to him about the place being called, "Sodom." When Mr. Finney arrived on the scene the building was filled to overflowing. The evangelist cried to God to give him the message that would make the deepest impression upon the hearts of the people that were present. The Lord, by his Spirit, gave him a strong suggestion that he should speak on the wickedness of Sodom. The evangelist obeyed the leading of the Lord and began to speak. He had not been speaking long until he noticed a strange commotion among the people. He tells of his experience as follows:

"I had not spoken to them more than a quarter of an hour, when all at once an awful solemnity seemed to settle down upon them; the congregation began to fall from their seats in every direction, and cried for mercy. If I had had a sword in each hand, I could not have

cut them off their seats as fast as they fell.
Indeed nearly the whole congregation were
either on their knees or prostrate, I should
think, in less than two minutes from this first
shock that fell upon them. Every one prayed
for himself, who was able to speak at all.

"Of course I was obliged to stop preaching;
for they no longer paid any attention. I saw
the old man who had invited me there to
preach, sitting about in the middle of the house,
and looking around with utter amazement. I
raised my voice almost to a scream, to make
him hear, and pointing to him said, 'Can't you
pray?' He instantly fell upon his knees, and
with a stentorian voice poured himself out to
God; but he did not at all get the attention of
the people. I then spake as loudly as I could,
and tried to make them attend to me. I said to
them, 'You are not in hell yet; and now let
me direct you to Christ.' For a few moments
I tried to hold forth the Gospel to them; but
scarcely any of them paid any attention. My
heart was so overflowing with joy at such a
scene that I could hardly contain myself. It
was with much difficulty that I refrained from
shouting, and giving glory to God.

"As soon as I could sufficiently control my
feelings I turned to a young man who was

close to me, and was engaged in praying for himself, laid my hand on his shoulder, thus getting his attention, and preached in his ear Jesus. As soon as I got his attention to the cross of Christ, he believed, was calm and quiet for a minute or two, and then broke out in praying for others. I then turned to another, and took the same course with him, with the same result; and then another, and another.

"There was too much interest, and there were too many wounded souls, to dismiss the meeting; and so it was held all night. In the morning there were still those there that could not get away; and they were carried to a private house in the neighborhood, to make room for the school. In the afternoon they sent for me to come down there, as they could not yet break up the meeting."

Sometimes the Spirit of God seemed to hover, in a very remarkable manner, over the community where many souls were being convicted and saved. In speaking of his revival meetings at Utica, New York, Mr. Finney says: "Our meetings were crowded every night, and the work went on powerfully. The place became filled with the manifest influence of the Holy Spirit."

A sheriff was converted who boarded at the

largest hotel in the place. Mr. Finney said: "That hotel became a centre of spiritual influence, and many were converted there. The stages, as they passed through, stopped at the hotel; and so powerful was the impression in the community, that I heard of several cases of persons that just stopped for a meal, or to spend a night, being powerfully convicted and converted before they left the town. Indeed, both in this place and in Rome (N. Y.), it was a common remark that nobody could be in the town, or pass through it, without being aware of the presence of God; that a divine influence seemed to pervade the place, and the whole atmosphere to be instinct with a divine life."

It was during the revival at Utica, New York, that the Spirit of God fell upon the workers of a large factory in a very extraordinary manner. Mr. Finney had conducted a meeting at the school house near the factory. A number of the employees attended the meeting and were deeply impressed. The next morning Mr. Finney went to visit the factory where his brother-in-law was the superintendent. In his autobiography he tells of the remarkable scene that followed:

"The next morning, after breakfast, I went into the factory, to look around it. As I went through, I observed there was a good deal of agitation among those who were busy at their looms, and their mules, and other implements of work. On passing through one of the apartments, where a great number of young women were attending to their weaving, I observed a couple of them eyeing me, and speaking very earnestly to each other; and I could see that they were a good deal agitated, although they both laughed. I went slowly toward them. They saw me coming, and were evidently much excited. One of them was trying to mend a broken thread, and I observed that her hands trembled so that she could not mend it. I approached slowly, looking on each side at the machinery, as I passed; but observed that this girl grew more and more agitated, and could not proceed with her work. When I came within eight or ten feet of her, I looked solemnly at her. She observed it, and was quite overcome, and sunk down, and burst into tears. The impression caught almost like powder, and in a few moments nearly all in the room were in tears. This feeling spread through the factory.

"Mr. W——, the owner of the establishment, was present, and seeing the state of things, he said to the superintendent, 'Stop the mill, and let the people attend to religion; for it is more important that our souls should be saved than that this factory run.' The gate was immediately shut down, and the factory stopped; but where should we assemble? The superintendent suggested that the mule room was large; and, the mules being run up, we could assemble there. We did so, and a more powerful meeting I scarcely ever attended. It went on with great power. The building was large, and had many people in it, from the garret to the cellar. The revival went through the mill with astonishing power, and in the course of a few days nearly all in the mill were hopefully converted."

Powerful revival meetings were conducted by Mr. Finney in Philadelphia and nearby cities. Multitudes were saved, and great numbers of Christians were wondrously quickened in the faith. During the meetings in Philadelphia some lumberman came down to the city from what was called the "lumber region," extending along the headwaters of the Delaware River. These visitors caught the revival fire and carried it back to the scattered lumbermen in the forests of the "lumber region."

A revival followed that was one of the most unique in the annals of evangelism. Mr. Finney tells how the fire spread among the scattered people living in the forests in that part of Pennsylvania. He said:

"These men that came down with lumber, attended our meetings, and quite a number of them were hopefully converted. They went back into the wilderness, and began to pray for the outpouring of the Holy Spirit, and to tell the people around them what they had seen in Philadelphia, and to exhort them to attend to their salvation. Their efforts were immediately blessed, and the revival began to take hold, and to spread among those lumbermen. It went on in a most powerful and remarkable manner. It spread to such an extent that in many cases persons would be convicted and converted, who had not attended any meetings, and who were almost as ignorant as heathen. Men who were getting out lumber, and were living in little shanties alone, or where two or three or more were together, would be seized with such conviction that it would lead them to wander off and inquire what they should do; and they would be converted, and thus the revival spread. There was the greatest simplicity manifested by the converts.

"Later two or three men from this lumber region came there to see me, and to inquire

how they could get some ministers to go in
there. They said that not less than five thousand people had been converted in that lumber
region; that the revival had extended itself
along for eighty miles, and there was not a
single minister of the gospel there."

Intercessory prayer was the very center and
cornerstone of the revival under Mr. Finney.
He said:

"Not only were prayer meetings greatly
multiplied and fully attended, not only was
there great solemnity in those meetings, but
there was a mighty spirit of secret prayer.
Christians prayed a great deal—many of them
would spend hours in private prayer. It was
also the case that two or more would take the
promise: 'If two of you shall agree on earth as
touching anything that they shall ask, it shall
be done for them of my Father which is in
heaven,' and make some particular person a
subject of prayer; and it was wonderful to what
an extent they prevailed. Answers to prayer
were so manifestly multiplied on every side,
that no one could escape the conviction that
God was daily and hourly answering prayer."

Finney further said: "If anything occurred
to threaten to hurt the work, if there was an
appearance of any root of bitterness springing

up, or any tendency to fanaticism or disorder, Christians would take the alarm, and give themselves to prayer that God would direct and control all things, and it was surprising to see to what extent, and by what means, God would remove obstacles out of the way in answer to prayer.

"Prayer is an essential link in the chain of causes that lead to a revival just as much as truth is. Some have zealously used truth to convert men, and laid very little stress upon prayer. They have preached, and talked, and distributed tracts with great zeal and then wondered why they had so little success. And the reason was that they had forgotten to use the other branch of the means, *effectual prayer*. They overlooked the fact that truth by itself will never produce the effect, without the Spirit of God, and that the Spirit is given in answer to earnest prayer."

On one occasion Finney went to Rochester, New York, to hold a series of revival meetings. Abel Cleary went to Rochester also, but not to attend the meetings. He rented a room and while Finney preached Abel Cleary prayed. He interceded with God in an agony for souls. The Spirit of God was poured out mightily upon that city. Practically every lawyer in

Rochester was converted.

The climax of the great awakening came in 1857. Noonday prayer meetings were started in New York, Philadelphia and other cities. Then the movement spread with lightning-like rapidity throughout the land. In Philadelphia it is said that three thousand people attended the noonday prayer meetings, and in Chicago some two thousand were in attendance day by day. In one of Mr. Finney's meetings in Boston a man arose and said: "I am from Omaha, in Nebraska. On my journey East I have found a continuous prayer meeting all the way. We call it two thousand miles from Omaha to Boston; and here was a prayer meeting about two thousand miles in extent."

The entire country was stirred by these noonday prayer meetings. In his "History of American Revivals" Mr. Beardsley said:

"Men of all classes and conditions attended the services. Capitalists and laborers, manufacturers and artisans, professional men, merchants and clerks, butchers and bakers, men from every walk in life were represented from day to day. Drayman would drive up to the curb stone and securing their teams, would enter the service long enough for the singing of a hymn or a season of prayer, and then be off to their work."

"Reporters were detailed to narrate the progress of the meetings. Startling headlines called the attention of the public to the latest 'Revival News' of the day, and for the time being, criminal trials, politics, casualties, etc., were overshadowed by the remarkable religious interest which had been awakened. At one time the New York dailies published several extras filled with accounts of the progress of the work in various parts of the land."

Rev. John Shearer in his book on "Old Time Revivals" says: "In answer to the Church's united cry, ascending from all parts of the land, the Spirit of God in a very quiet way, and suddenly, throughout the whole extent of the United States, renewed the Church's life, and awakened in the community around it a great thirst for God. When the Church awoke to the full consciousness of the miracle, it found that from east and west, and from north and south, the whole land was alive with daily prayer meetings. And it was in these daily united prayer meetings that the great majority of these conversions, of all ages and classes, took place.

"The divine fire appeared in the most un-likely quarters. A large number of the aged were gathered in. White-haired penitents knelt with little children at the Throne of Grace. Whole families of Jews were brought to their Messiah. Deaf mutes were reached by the glad tidings, and though their tongues were still, their faces so shone that they became effective messengers of the gospel. The most hardened infidels were melted, some being led to Christ by the hand of a little child.

"Nor was the blessing confined to the land. The Spirit of God moved upon the face of the water, and a multitude of seamen saw a great light. It was as if a vast cloud of blessing hovered over the land and sea. And ships, as they drew near the American ports, came within the zone of heavenly influence. Ship after ship arrived with the same tale of sudden conviction and conversion. It was wonderful beyond words! In one ship a captain and the entire crew of thirty men found Christ out at sea and entered the harbor rejoicing.

"The North Carolina—a battleship of the United States Navy—lay in the harbor of New York. Her complement was about a thousand men. Amongst these were four Christians who discovered their spiritual kinship and agreed to meet for prayer. They were permitted to use a very retired part of the ship, on a deck far below the water line. Here, then, they gathered one evening. They were only four men, but they were a united band. They represented three denominations, one being an Episcopalian, another a Presbyterian, while two were Baptists.

"As they knelt in the dim light of a tiny lamp, the Spirit of God suddenly filled their hearts with such joy of salvation that they burst into song. The strange sweet strain rose to the decks above, and there created great astonishment. Their ungodly shipmates came running down. They came to mock, but the mighty power of God had been liberated by rejoicing faith. It gripped them, and in one moment their derisive laugh was changed into the cry of penitent sinners! Great fellows, giants in stature, and many of them giants in sin, were literally smitten down, and knelt humbly beside the four, like little children.

"A most gracious work straightway began in the depths of the great ship. Night after night the prayer meeting was held, and conversions took place daily. Soon they had to send ashore for help, and ministers joyfully came out to assist. A large number were added to the various churches, and the battleship became a veritable House of God! The North

Carolina was a receiving ship, from which men were constantly drafted to other ships.

"The converts of the revival were scattered throughout the navy. A revival convert is a burning brand. The holy fire spread rapidly from ship to ship. Wherever the converts went they started a prayer meeting and became a soul-winning band. Thus ship after ship left the harbor of New York for foreign seas, each carrying its band of rejoicing converts, and the fire of God was borne to the ends of the earth."

Dr. Beardsley in his History of American Revivals speaks of the numerical results of the revival of 1857: "For a period of six to eight weeks, when the revival was at its height, it was estimated that fifty thousand persons were converted weekly throughout the country, and as the revival lasted for more than a year, it becomes evident that the sum total of conversions reached a figure that was enormous. Conservative judges have placed the number of converts, in this great spiritual awakening, at five hundred thousand."

As we marvel at these glorious results, let us not fail to remember that they came to pass in response to a great volume of intercessory prayer!

Chapter III

WHEN THE FIRE FELL
IN IRELAND

There were four young men in Ireland whose hearts were burdened for the salvation of souls. They believed in the power of prayer, and met together for united earnest intercession for revival. The story of George Müller, and his great orphanage at Bristol, England, supported entirely in answer to believing prayer, quickened the faith of the young men. They began to believe that God could and would do mighty things in answer to their prayers.

Others also, who longed for revival, joined this prayer band, and they began to see definite conversions in answer to their intercession. Then came the news of the great revival in the United States, and the faith of the members of the prayer group was still further strengthened.

They heard that in New York City large numbers of business men met daily for prayer. Like Jacob of old, the young men cried out:

"I will not let Thee go, except Thou bless me." They believed the Word of God in Matthew 18:19 and 20: "Again I say unto you, That if two of you shall agree on earth as touching any thing that they shall ask, it shall be done for them of my Father which is in heaven. For where two or three are gathered together in my name, there am I in the midst of them."

Prayer meetings in Ireland began to multiply, and people were being saved daily. Then the fire fell from heaven! John Shearer in his book "Old Time Revivals" tells what happened: "A great revival is like a forest fire. At first there is only a thin line of flame. But soon its progress is so swift and widely diffused that the eye can no longer keep pace with it. The flame bursts forth at once in many places, and now we see but one great conflagration. So it was with this marvelous work of grace. You might observe its course in Connor and a little beyond in 1858. But in 1859 the heavenly fire was leaping up and spreading in all directions through Antrim, Downs, Derry, Tyrone, and the other counties of Ulster, and to this day '59' is remembered as the pre-eminent year of grace.

"As it advanced, it burned with a fierce intensity. In Connor the conversions were of a comparatively quiet type. But in Ahoghill, Ballymena, and elsewhere, there was a great smiting down. Sin was felt as a crushing and intolerable burden, and men and women often fell to the earth and continued for days in a state of utter prostration. Others were suddenly pierced as by a sharp sword, and their agonized cry for help was heard in the streets and in the fields. Here, for example, is a farmer returning from market in Ballymena. His mind is wholly intent upon the day's bargain. He pauses, takes out some money, and begins to count it. Suddenly an awful Presence envelopes him. In a moment his only thought is that he is a sinner standing on the brink of hell. His silver is scattered, and he falls upon the dust of the highway, crying out for mercy.

"There was a wonderful work amongst the children. The blessing had come to Coleraine, and one day the school master observed a boy so troubled that he was quite unfit for lessons. He kindly sent him home in the company of an older boy who had already found peace. As the two lads went on their way they saw an empty house, and went into it for prayer.

"While they knelt the painful burden lifted

from the boy's heart. He sprang to his feet in a transport of joy. Returning to the school, he ran up to the master and, with a beaming face, cried out, 'Oh, I am so happy! I have the Lord Jesus in my heart.' The effect of these artless words was very great. Boy after boy rose and silently left the room. In a little while the master followed and discovered his boys ranged alongside the wall of the playground, every one apart and on his knees!

"Very soon their silent prayer became a bitter cry. It was heard by those within and pierced their hearts. They cast themselves upon their knees, and their cry for mercy was heard in the girls' schoolroom above. In a few moments the whole school was upon its knees, and its wail of distress was heard in the street.

"Neighbors and passers-by came flocking in, and, as they crossed the threshold, came under the same convicting power. Every room was filled with men, women, and children seeking God. The ministers of the town and men of prayer were sent for, and the whole day was spent in directing these mourners to the Lord Jesus. That school proved to be for many the house of God and the very gate of heaven.

"It pleased God to use in a very remarkable manner the simple testimony of the four young

men of Connor. Through them the revival
reached Belfast. Of a sudden, ministers who
had toiled in vain for years found themselves
surrounded by sin-sick souls clamoring for the
life-giving Word. But for the co-operation of
Sabbath School teachers and other friends
they would speedily have been exhausted with
the work. Vast and memorable gatherings
were held. Districts notorious as the scenes of
party strife, witnessed the triumph of the gospel of peace. Bitter opponents knelt together
at the Saviour's feet. Belfast became like a
city of God."

The awakening that followed was indeed
extraordinary. It was the greatest spiritual
quickening that the land had witnessed for
generations. Visitors from many lands flocked
to Ireland to witness the great awakening.
Churches were filled to overflowing. The hearts
of the ministers sang for joy as they saw
sinners in an agony of soul under the convicting power of the Holy Spirit; then burst-
ing forth into ecstatic joy as they found par-
don and peace; and going forth with the light
of heaven on their faces to tell others the glad
tidings.

A stirring history of the revival was written
by Professor William Gibson, the moderator

of the Presbyterian Church in Ireland. It is a book of some 500 pages. It is filled with authentic stories of large numbers of people who were converted during the revival. In speaking of how the awakening started in a quiet corner of Ireland, and spread rapidly here and there, Professor Gibson says: "In startling and impressive grandeur it burst forth in a comparatively sequestered region; and scarcely had the new-born flame, drawn down by a few earnest watchers there, begun to burn, when it spread in all directions over an entire province. All classes and all ages caught the heavenly fire."

The fact that there were "some temporary excesses and extravagancies" in connection with the revival did not trouble Professor Gibson. He asked, who at such a time would criticise or "grudge to these new-gathered souls the overflowing fulness of their joy?"

As is so often the case in revivals the converts of one place carried the fire to other communities. Rev. A. J. Canning of Coleraine, Ireland, tells how the awakening came to that town: "Upon the evening of the 7th of June, 1859, an open-air meeting was held in one of the market-places of the town, called 'Fair-Hill.' The announced object of the meeting was to receive and hear one or two of the 'converts,' as they began to be called, from a district some eight or ten miles south of Coleraine. The evening was one of the most lovely that ever shone. The richly wooded banks of the river Bann, which bounds one side of the square in which the meeting was held, were fully in prospect, and there was not a cloud in the sky.

"Shortly after seven o'clock, dense masses of people, from town and country, began to pour into the square by all its approaches, and in a short time an enormous multitude crowded around the platform from which speakers were to address the meeting. After singing and prayer, the converts, a young man and a man more advanced in years, and both of the humbler class, proceeded to address the meeting. Their addresses were short, and consisted almost entirely of a detail of their own awakening, and earnest appeals to the consciences of sinners. After the lapse of nearly an hour, it became manifest that more than one-half of the congregated multitude could not hear the voices of the speakers on the platform. Then it was suggested that the people should separate into distinct congregations or groups, and that a minister should preach to each group.

This was immediately done, and some three or four separate audiences were soon listening with most marked attention to as many preachers, for all the ministers of all the evangelical churches in the town were present.

"I was engaged in addressing a large group of people, composed of all ages and of all ranks of the community, from a portion of Scripture, when I became struck with the deep and peculiar attention which every mind and heart was lending to what I said. As to manner, my address was very calm; as to matter, it consisted of plain gospel truth, as it concerns man's lost condition on the one hand, and the free grace of God, as displayed in salvation, on the other. I know that the addresses of my brethren were of a like character. I never saw before, in any audience, the same searching, earnest, riveted look fixed upon my face, as strained up to me from almost every eye in that hushed and apparently awe-struck multitude. I remember, even whilst I was speaking, asking myself, 'How is this? why is this?' As yet, however, the people stood motionless, and perfectly silent.

"About the time the last speaker was closing his address, a very peculiar cry arose from out a dense group at one side of the square, and in less than ten minutes a similar cry was repeated in six or eight different groups, until, in a very short time, the whole multitude was divided into awe-struck assemblages around persons prostrate on the ground, or supported in the arms of relatives or friends.

"I hurried to the center of one of these groups, and having first exhorted the persons standing around to retire, and leave me to deal with the prostrate one, I stooped over him, and found him to be a young man of some eighteen or twenty years, but personally unknown to me. He lay on the ground, his head supported on the knees of an elder of one of our churches. His eyes were closed; his hands were firmly clasped, and occasionally very forcibly pressed upon the chest. He was uttering incessantly a peculiar deep moan, sometimes terminating in a prolonged wailing cry.

"I felt his pulse, and could discern nothing very peculiar about it. I said, softly and quietly in his ear, 'Why do you cry so?' when he opened his eyes for an instant, and I could perceive that they had, stronger than I ever saw it before, that inward look, which indicates that the mind is wholly occupied with its own images and impressions. 'Oh!' he exclaimed, high and loud, in reply to my question, 'my

sins! my sins! Lord Jesus, have mercy upon
my poor soul! O Jesus! come! O Lord Jesus,
come !'

"I endeavored to calm him for a moment,
asking him to listen to me whilst I set before
him some of the promises of God to perishing
sinners. At first I thought that I was carrying
his attention with me in what I was saying,
but I soon discovered that his whole soul was
filled with one idea—his guilt and his danger—
for, in the middle of my repetition of some
promise, he would burst forth with the bitter
cry, 'O God, my sins! my sins!' At length I
said in his ear, 'Shall I pray?' He replied in a
loud voice, 'Oh, yes!' I engaged in prayer, and
yet I doubt whether his mind followed me
beyond the first sentence or two.'

"As I arose from prayer, six or eight persons, all at the same instant, pressed around
me, crying, 'Oh, come and see (naming such
a one—and—and)'—until I felt for a moment
bewildered, and the prayer went out from my
own heart, 'God guide me!' I passed from
case to case for two or three hours, as did my
brethren in the ministry, until, when the night
was far spent, and the stricken ones began to
be removed to the shelter of roofs, I turned
my face homewards through one street, when

I soon discovered that the work which had begun in the market-square was now advancing with marvellous rapidity in the homes of the people. As I approached door after door, persons were watching for me and other ministers, to bring us to deal with some poor agonized stricken one; and when the morning dawned, and until the sun arose, I was wandering from street to street, and from house to house, on the most marvelous and solemn errand upon which I have ever been sent."

An eye-witness of the revival in Ballymena says: "It was in the opening summer that the revival came, when the light lingers so long at nightfall, and the bright mornings break so soon. We can remember how many lighted windows there were though the night was far gone, and how prayer-meetings were prolonged till the day had returned again. Every evening the churches were crowded, and family worship became almost universal. In the country, large meetings were held in the open air. Part of the dinner-hour was generally devoted to singing and prayer, and the sound from numerous groups of worshipers could be heard far at a distance as it was borne on the summer breeze. Thousands of tracts were circulated and read with avidity, and long-neglected Bibles came into general use.

"When the great outpouring came, worldly men were silent with an indefinite fear, and Christians found themselves borne onward in the current, with scarce time for any feeling but the overpowering conviction that a great revival had come at last. Careless men were bowed in unaffected earnestness, and sobbed like children. Drunkards and boasting blasphemers were awed into solemnity. Sabbath-school teachers and scholars became seekers of Christ together; and languid believers were stirred up to unusual exertion. Ministers who had often toiled in heartfelt sorrow suddenly found themselves beset by inquirers, and wholly unequal to the demands which were made. Every day many were hopefully converted, passing through an ordeal of conviction more or less severe, to realize their great deliverance, and to throw themselves with every energy into the work of warning others, or of leading them to the Lord. All this came suddenly."

The revival was not a mere emotional upheaval. The work of God's Spirit was deep and lasting. Rev. John Stuart tells of the revival in a place not far from Coleraine: "Never was there such a summer as the last; never

such an autumn; never such a winter, so far as
it has gone. Hundreds have been savingly
converted to the Lord; some 'stricken' down
when the Spirit came upon them like a 'rushing mighty wind'; others convinced and converted whilst He spake to their consciences by
the 'still small voice.' The first effect of the
revival was, that 'fear came upon every soul.'
Then our church was filled to suffocation, and
we were obliged to take to the open fields to
declare the message of mercy to a hungering
and thirsting population. The hitherto unoc-
cupied pews were ardently sought after. The
aisles were filled with anxious hearers, and now
preaching became a luxury. I had pastor's
work to do. I had living men and living women
before me. They came to the sanctuary on the
sole errand of obtaining the 'bread of life.'
Every Sabbath was a day of 'sweet refresh-
ing.' On every week-day evening 'they that
feared the Lord spake often one to another,
and the Lord hearkened and heard,' and 'there
were added to the church daily such as should
be saved.' Of all the stricken ones—two hundred in number—I do not know of one back-
slider."

Chapter IV

THE REVIVAL FIRE SPREADS

The revival rapidly spread from place to place in northern Ireland. In homes, in churches, in open-air meetings, people came under the influence of the heavenly flame, and found their lives transformed by a new power that flooded their souls with heavenly glory.

In one district not far from Dundrod there was a young man of wild and reckless habits who treated the revival with scorn. He was so much opposed to the movement that he forbade his sisters to go too near the meetings lest they should bring the plague home with them. But he himself soon became one of the most zealous of the revival converts.

There was a girl who had been converted in the Dundrod meetings. She was now filled with a great love for the lost and a great desire to lead them to Christ. This girl went from house to house pleading with the unsaved to accept Christ. In a providential manner she was led to the home of this young scoffer. She pled with him with gentle, but intense earnestness. She implored him to pray.

Presently, under the influence of the Spirit of God, the young man softened and began to yield. Now let the revival narrator tell the rest of the story:

"Now, they are on their knees together; while father and mother, and sisters and brothers, stand awhile in wonder, then kneel too, and all pray earnestly. The young man struggles, feels a choking sensation in his throat, and a pressure on his heart; his bosom heaves with strange emotions. The strong man is bowed down, the hard heart is softening, the Spirit is striving; and now the struggle is over, and another Saul stands up. Rejoicing in his new-born freedom, he asks for work, saying, 'Lord, what wilt thou have me to do?' The work is given, and with all his heart he sets about doing it.

"In his family he begins, and soon all the members of the household are changed; father, mother, sisters, and brothers—blessing God for bringing salvation into their home. Now he goes in haste to rouse his sleeping neighbors and friends. He stands up in the midst of hundreds in the open-air meetings proclaiming the glad tidings of salvation, and glorying in the possession of a light, and life, and joy, never felt nor dreamed of before.

"He seeks his old companions, whom he led in many a revel; and on the following Sabbath, in the face of the most crowded and solemn assembly ever held among us, he marches up at the head of nearly one hundred individuals, who in front of the pulpit, sign the total abstinence pledge. His mission does not end here. He and others visit from house to house, hold prayer-meetings, and the revival spreads around until every family in the district can count its converts; and in more than one instance whole families 'joy in God, through the Lord Jesus Christ, by whom they have received the atonement.'

"There is life now in the people, a new, a spiritual life. The Spirit has quickened hundreds who were 'dead in trespasses and sins.' The cry is heard on all sides, 'Such times, such glorious times! the Lord indeed is come among us.' Prayers issue from lips that never moved in audible prayer before; and oh, such prayers! so rich in Scripture language, so fervent, for icy hearts are melted as if by fire from heaven. Men and women pray; father follows a son, or a sister, or a brother. They are resolved to take heaven by force, and not to yield until they themselves, and their friends, stand within the city of God.

"Prayer-meetings are appointed in the several districts of the congregation, but wherever there is an earnest seeking soul, the people meet for prayer. The songs of Zion ascend from almost every house. And in the still summer evening, strains of heavenly music seem to float on the tremulous air. Imagination is busy, and no wonder, as men pause on the highway to catch the sweet sounds, now soft and low, rising and falling, and now ringing like the chimes of church-bells. They thought the angels were above and around them. They thought they heard the festive chimes of heaven, the pealing of the bells in the city of God, as the heavenly host proclaimed the triumphs which their Lord was achieving over his foes on the earth.

> 'Hark, how they sweetly sing,
> Worthy is our Saviour King;
> Loud, let his praises ring,
> Praise, praise for aye.'

The Spirit of God came upon people right in their own homes, and sometimes they were thrown into an agony of remorse for their sins. Rev. J. M. Killen of Comber tells of one such case:

"An elderly woman, the mother of a family,

who had been a careless, cursing creature, and one greatly opposed to the revival, was suddenly and violently prostrated on her own kitchen floor. When I first saw her she was rolling on the ground and writhing with agony. Her appearance was certainly the most satanic I ever beheld. The bystanders were overawed; all felt that influences more than human were at work. A medical man was sent for, but he fled at the sight, declaring that it was a case for a clergyman, and not for a physician. The unhappy woman was evidently the subject of a great spiritual conflict. Her cries for about an hour were terrific. She declared that Satan and all the devils in hell were round about her.

"Gradually her shrieks subsided, and as the paroxysms wore off, she settled down into a sort of despairing calm. For days she continued weak in body and distressed in soul. But at length the light broke, her bonds were loosed, she saw and embraced Christ, obtained peace, and was filled with a joy unspeakable and full of glory. And she is now one of the finest specimens of Christian character, and of a mother in Israel, I have ever known—distinguished by her strong faith, her ardent love, and her Christian meekness, her sweetness of temper, and an almost uninterrupted realization of her Redeemer's presence, combined with a very profound reverence for Messiah's character, a strong desire to promote his glory, and a most extreme sensitiveness lest she should do anything to forfeit the enjoyment of his love. 'O Sir,' said she lately to me, 'I am just watching how I lift and lay down my feet, lest I should offend Him.'"

As was natural in such a spiritual awakening the public-houses (saloons) lost many of their customers, while some of them were closed entirely. A minister who took an active part in the revival tells how one of the largest public-houses in his district was closed:

"The owner did a large business, and was making money fast. He had a wife and rising family to support. But he had a conscience, and had for some time felt uneasy and unhappy in his mind because he could not reconcile his profession as a Christian with his trade as a publican (saloon-keeper). He told me, that even before the revival, he could not, with profit, sit under my ministry, and dared not go to the Lord's table while engaged in such an accursed business.

"The revival came. It roused his conscience afresh, and it gave him no rest. In his neigh-

borhood, particularly in one house, were many
cases of conviction, and many meetings. He
attended them all; saw, and heard, and
judged for himself.

"He said to me one morning, 'I want to
consult you about this business of mine; I
don't like it—I have long felt unhappy in it—
I will give it up. Shall I do so now—or wait
until I sell out my stock?'

"I gave him my opinion, and on that same
evening every puncheon of whiskey, and bar-
rel of beer and ale, every bottle and glass, and
every article used in the trade had disappeared; and on the next morning I saw their
vacant spaces filled with barrels and bags of
meal and flour, sides of bacon, etc. This was
a noble triumph. Dagon had fallen before the
ark of God. One fountain of evil was closed
forever.

"Great was the amazement of the traveler,
when he called the next day for his customary
glass. He opens his eyes, and stares and wonders. And 'still his wonder grows' when he
steps out of the shop and finds that the sign-
board is gone. ' 'Tis strange, passing strange!
either God or the devil is here.' Some say, 'He
is gone mad like the rest. He has been be-
witched; he has taken the revival.' He has,

indeed, and has therefore renounced the devil
and all his works.

"Afterward in the public meeting, men
heartily joined in the prayer from the pulpit,
'God bless him, and reward him an hundred-
fold'; and God heard the prayer, and he is
blessed, and rejoices in the smiles of an ap-
proving conscience, and is thankful for the
grace which enabled him to trample on self
and sin. This case gave a great impulse to the
whole movement. Another public-house soon
closed its doors, and a third, and now the only
one in the neighborhood, gets almost nothing
to do."

The ministers of northern Ireland did not
simply stand by, and watch the revival fire
spread from place to place. They took active
steps to promote the movement. Rev. Robert
Wallace, a Wesleyan minister, of Derry, told
of some of the means used to fan the revival
flame: "Early in the summer, arrangements
were made to bring down from Ballymena
and Ballymoney a number of those who had
been recently brought under gracious influence, and it was agreed that they should take
part in the public services in the Presbyterian
and Wesleyan Churches, and also in the open
air at the market-place. At these services

great crowds attended. The persons recently awakened spoke with great simplicity of the wonderful change that God had wrought in them, by grace, in the course of the last few weeks or days. A solemn awe rested upon the people. At the commencement of the meetings, a number of ministers, representing various denominations, met by request at the house of the senior Presbyterian minister, and arranged plans for combined efforts to promote the cause of God; and in this manner a service was held in the market-place every evening throughout the summer. The utmost unity prevailed, and this greatly tended to deepen the interest among the people."

One of the chroniclers of the revival wrote: "When I visited one district, I found that all labor was completely suspended, and that all the people were running in groups from house to house. In some houses, at one time, I counted more than a score, old and young, more or less affected. The people here seemed to 'take it' with wonderful rapidity. There was a regular chain of meetings kept up night and day, each meeting feeding the flame of zeal, and from each, as from a burning altar, live coals were taken to touch the cold lips and fire the dead souls of the few 'careless ones' elsewhere."

Another eye-witness of the awakening tells
of the change that took place among the employees of a mill when one of them was converted and resolved to "pray through" for
his ungodly work-mates: "A poor man, advanced in life and unmarried, was converted
in our congregation at the beginning of the
work. As soon as he himself had embraced the
Lord, he became most anxious for the conversion of the family with whom he resided, and
of his fellow-workmen in the mill where he
was employed. But all these were most ungodly; and when they saw the change which
had taken place in him, instead of rejoicing in his joy, they mocked, swore, sang im-
pure songs, and did all they could to thwart
and distress him. He saw that remonstrances
were vain, and he resolved to pray for them.
He did so, but for a time no answer came, and
he was sorely discouraged. Still he resolved to
continue his supplications on their behalf.
Then suddenly one day the men in the mill
were astonished at cries proceeding from their
homes, which were nearby. The business in the
mill was suspended, and the men rushed to
their houses to see what had caused the cries.
They found their wives and daughters pros-

trated under strong conviction, crying to the Lord for mercy. The hitherto despised convert was at once appealed to, and, with a heart overflowing with gratitude, he led their supplications and directed all to Christ. Soon the Lord vouchsafed His mercy; the weeping penitents became rejoicing converts, and wives and daughters were that day added to the Lord.

"But his prayers were as yet only partially answered. They were soon to receive a more glorious fulfilment. Some days after the above occurrence, the mill had again to be stopped, but this time not because of the women, but the men. Husbands and brothers, whilst engaged at their work, were arrested and smitten down whilst in the very act of attending the machinery. Some of the strongest men and greatest scoffers in the whole country fell powerless in a moment under the mighty and mysterious influence that was at work.

"Never had there been such a day in that establishment. Strong men were seen prostrated and crying for mercy. Converted wives and daughters bent over them with tears of joy, whilst they returned thanks to God for the awakening of their husbands and brothers, and prayed that soon all might rejoice

with one another as heirs together of the grace
of life. And such has been the case. The poor
man's prayers have indeed been answered. He
has just been telling me that the seven souls
in the house where he resides are now all converted, and that about nine-tenths of the
workers in the mill have been visited by the
Spirit of the Lord."

The same chronicler tells of the change that
came to the men of a stone-quarry when the
Spirit of God fell upon them: "Near the outskirts of the parish, there is a quarry, which
was formerly notorious for the wickedness of
those who wrought in it. It was, in fact an
emporium for all sorts of vice; but when our
revival commenced in Comber, it was such a
strange and unheard-of thing among these
quarrymen, that they resolved, through curi-
osity, to come and see it. They accordingly
attended the nightly prayer-meetings in our
congregation. Gradually a change crept over
them. Drinking was diminished, swearing was
given up, seriousness and anxiety prevailed.
I was requested to go and preach to them
during working hours in the middle of the
day. I did so. Immediately on my appearance
all work was suspended; and, at the very busi-
est time, master and men attended for up-

wards of two hours. Under the open sky, in a sort of large amphitheatre, formed by the excavation of the quarry, and surrounded by the mountain's rocky walls, I proclaimed to them the glorious gospel of the blessed God.

"Prayer-meetings amongst the men were immediately established. The head of the quarry soon announced to his men that he himself was entirely changed, and declared that he had resolved to live henceforth only for Christ. A marvelous transformation was soon apparent among the men. The head of the establishment told me that out of ninety-six families in his employment, upwards of ninety have now established family worship. 'Drunkenness,' he said, 'has disappeared, and neither oath nor improper expression is now heard in that quarry. As for myself,' he continued, 'I consider myself as a mere steward, having nothing of my own, and bound by feelings, both of responsibility and gratitude, to live for God's glory.'"

The results of the revival were deep and permanent and far-reaching. The awakening brought a new era of grace and glory to the churches of northern Ireland. One of the ministers wrote: "After examining the facts as far as I could gather them, I judge that

not less than one hundred thousand persons
in Ulster were brought under gracious influence during that time. The revival had the
help of almost the entire secular press. It was
not confined to any one denomination, but
embraced all evangelical churches; and up till
the present time, all those have maintained an
unprecedented unity. I consider it the most
glorious work of God ever known in this country in so short a time."

CHAPTER V

WHEN THE FIRE FELL IN WALES

The results of the revival in Ireland were long and lasting. Ministers and laymen looked back with profound gratitude to God for the glorious awakening of '59.

After a period of forty-five years the fire again fell from heaven—this time in Wales. Once more there was a mighty outpouring of God's Spirit. Vast multitudes were saved, and the Christians of the land were wondrously quickened in the faith.

For the time being Wales became the spiritual center of Christendom. Visitors from many lands flocked to Wales to witness the revival meetings, hoping, if possible, to carry back some of the revival fire to their own countries. Revival was the chief topic of conversation. The Welsh newspapers devoted columns to the movement each day; and occasionally special Revival Editions were issued.

A Chicago publisher, Mr. S. B. Shaw, was so stirred by the news of the great awakening in Wales that he compiled a very interesting book containing eye-witness reports of the revival, which had appeared in various religious papers in Great Britain and America. The book was entitled "The Great Revival in Wales." It was published forty years ago. Providentially some copies were preserved by the publishers throughout the past decades and recently came into the possession of Mr. C. F. Chapman, of Jacksonville, Florida, who is earnestly praying and working for another great spiritual awakening in our land.

Mr. Chapman kindly sent me a copy of the book, and from it I received great spiritual blessing and also much helpful material. I praise God for leading Mr. Shaw to gather so many interesting incidents about the revivals in Wales and Ireland, and I am deeply grateful to Mr. Chapman for sending me a copy of the book. How marvelously God works His wonders to perform!

Here is a vivid description of the revival in Wales that appeared in a religious paper in Chicago at the time of the great awakening:

"A wonderful revival is sweeping over Wales. The whole country, from the city to the colliery underground, is aflame with gospel glory. Police courts are hardly necessary, public houses are being deserted, old debts are being paid to satisfy awakened consciences, and definite and unmistakable answers to prayer are recorded.

"The leader in this great religious movement is a young man twenty-six years of age, Evan Roberts. First he worked in a coal mine, then became an apprentice in a forge, then a student for the ministry. But all his life he has yearned to preach the gospel. He is no orator, he is not widely read. The only book he knows from cover to cover is the Bible. He has in his possession a Bible which he values above anything else belonging to him. It is a Bible slightly scorched in a colliery explosion. When the evangelist was working in a colliery he used to take his Bible with him, and while at work would put it away in some convenient hole or nook near his working place, ready to his hand when he could snatch a moment or two to scan its beloved pages. A serious explosion occurred one day. The future Welsh revivalist escaped practically unhurt, but the leaves of his Bible were scorched by the fiery blast. 'Evan Roberts' scorched Bible' is a familiar phrase among his friends.

"Little more than a month ago Evan Roberts was unknown, studying in one of the Welsh colleges at Newcastle-Emlyn to prepare for the Calvinistic Methodist ministry. Then came the summons, and he obeyed. He insists that he has been called to his present work by the direct guidance of the Holy Ghost. At once, without question and without hesitation, he was accepted by the people. Wherever he went hearts were set aflame with the love of God.

"The dominant note of the revival is prayer and praise. Another striking fact is the joyousness and radiant happiness of the evangelist. Evan Roberts smiles when he prays, laughs when he preaches. 'Ah, it is a grand life,' he cries. 'I am happy, so happy that I could walk on the air. Tired? Never! God has made me strong. He has given me courage.'

"He is a leader who preaches victory, and shows how it may be won—victory over the dull depression and gloomy doubt of our time. It has long been felt in Wales as elsewhere, that the time was ripe for a great religious revival. As the Rev. H. M. Hughes, a Congregational minister in Cardiff, recently pointed out, all efforts, movements, and organizations did not stem the flood of evil or stop the growth of pleasure-seeking and mammon worship. A generation had risen that had not seen the arm of God working as it had done in 1859 in Ireland.

"Now, the revival has arrived, and it has many of the marks of previous great awakenings. Strong men are held in its grip; the Spirit of God stirs to their very depths whole neighborhoods and districts. There is a tumult of emotion, an overpowering influence, and a conviction of sin that can only be attributed to Divine agency.

"Personal eloquence, magnetism, fervor, or mental power do not account for it. The only explanation is the one which the evangelist gives—it is all of God. And it has already done infinite good in places far away from its immediate locality. Men everywhere are thinking, talking, discussing religious topics, and at last God, Christ, and the soul have to some degree come to their own. The revival seems to work especially among young people. Its form is that of prayer, praise, and personal testimony. Its absence of method makes it the expression of the emotions of young hearts aflame with the love of God."

In an article on the revival in the Methodist Times of London, England, Rev. T. Ferrier Hulme records some of the impressions of his visit to Wales to see the awakening: "It will give us all renewed faith in prayer, for this is emphatically a praying revival. Evan Roberts told me that prayer became so passionate and mighty at Caerphilly that at midnight a number of men formed themselves into a 'Get-them-out-of-bed brigade,' and, in an hour or two, three of the sinners prayed for became so miserable in bed that they dressed hurriedly, and came on to the service, and yielded to Christ there and then. I have seen over and over again the complete abandonment with which men give themselves up to pleading, as if they were totally unconscious of any presence but that of Christ, and are quite unaffected by anything or anybody else. Even when I could not understand a single word I have been indescribably moved.

"Extraordinary incidents are as numerous as ever. At Cardiff a young man, who had been lost to his parents for three years, turned up at the very service where his father (a county magistrate) and his mother were praying for him. His father knelt at his side to help him to Jesus, but the son did not recognize him till they both rose to give praise! They then went together to find the mother, who in another part of the chapel was earnestly praying for her lost boy, and was totally oblivious of anything and any one around her.

The scene was indescribably pathetic, and the joy of all was ecstatic.

"What was and is remarkable right throughout the meetings is their spontaneity. On some occasions as many as half a dozen commence to pray at one time, and continually brothers and sisters are on their feet to pray, waiting turns. One old brother six times attempted to pray and each time was forestalled by someone else.

"It was a glorious sight to see sinners rising and coming to the penitent form seeking forgiveness. After the singing of 'Come to Jesus,' the question was asked, 'Who will come to Him now?' A man got up and shouted, 'I will,' and then broke down. Then his wife came out to the penitent form, and all his children. Another case occurred during the singing of 'Throw Out the Life-Line.' A passer-by who was drunk was so affected by the singing that he turned into the meeting. It was wonderful to see the change that took place in him before the meeting was over. He came forward and confessed Christ, and when the meeting closed he was a sober man. Never has the Spirit of God been felt in such a powerful manner before.

"Many who have long been prayed for have

yielded; backsliders have come back, and many wonderful cases of conversion have taken place. The football field, the dance, and the dramatic entertainment have been given up, and many things laid aside for the 'revival meetings.' "

Another report in the Methodist Times tells of the decrease in drunkenness and crime, as the result of the revival: "Reports from all the districts in South Wales affected by the revival show that the Christmas holidays, so dreaded by new converts who formerly devoted the whole of the time to drink and revelry, have passed by without the defections from the faith which were loudly prophesied by the unsympathetic and unbelieving. South Wales has never known such a quiet and peaceful Christmas.

"In Cardiff, police reports show that drunkenness has diminished over 60 per cent, whilst on Saturday last the Mayor was presented by the Chief Constable with a pair of white gloves, there being no case at all on the charge sheet—an unprecedented fact for the last day of the year.

"The same thing happened at the Swansea County Court on the previous Saturday, and the magistrate said, 'In all the years I've been sitting here I've never seen anything like it, and I attribute this happy state of things entirely to the revival.'

"The streets of Aberdare on Christmas Eve were almost entirely free from drunkenness, and on Christmas Day there were no prisoners at all in the cells. At Abercarn Police Court, responsible for a population of 21,000, there was not a single summons on Thursday—a thing unknown since the court was formed fourteen years ago—and here, too, was enacted the ceremony of the white gloves.

"The change in the language of the crowds has been just as marked as the change in their drinking habits. As the old hymn says:

> Suffice that for the season past
> Hell's horrid language filled our tongues,
> We all Thy words behind us cast,
> And lewdly sang the drunkard's songs.
>
> But, O the power of grace divine!
> In hymns we now our voices raise,
> Loudly in strange hosannas join,
> And blasphemies are turned to praise!

"Whilst bands of enthusiastic workers have paraded the streets, arresting the attention of the careless by joyful song and earnest invitation, homely meetings have been extemporized in cottages, and here some of the most precious experiences of the revival have been obtained. At one of these family gatherings no less than five conversions were recorded.

"The secular press is still fanning the flame by its sympatheitc reports of the revival meetings. Surely one of the most remarkable facts yet recorded in daily journalism is the 'Revival Edition' of the Evening Express, published in Cardiff. The managers had found a football edition paid them well; so they experimented with a 'Revival Edition,' in which every article, every report, every paragraph, and every portrait, indeed every line, except the advertisements, dealt with religious work. It has had such an enormous sale that a similar edition was produced last Tuesday."

Another report of the revival tells of the great increase in the sale of New Testaments and Bibles, and a corresponding decrease in the sale of low-class literature: "The Welsh are supposed to be a Bible-reading people, and judging by the numerous and apt quotations in their prayers they know a great deal more about the contents of the Book than the average man. And yet again and again when Evan Roberts has tested the congregations it was found that even among Christian people Bible readers were in a minority. Those who have confessed their neglect have promised to amend their ways, and they have so far kept their vow by purchasing Bibles in large quantities.

"The increase in the sales has been very great. A bookseller at Ton, in the heart of the Rhondda, who has been eighteen years in the trade, says the increase has been 'tremendous' —and there has been a corresponding decrease in the sale of low-class literature. So say two booksellers in the neighboring town of Pentre, who add that the most remarkable increase has been in the purchase of pocket Testaments by young men. At Neath a bookseller states that before the revival he regarded Bibles as dead stock, but in recent weeks he had cleared out all his old stock and has had to get further supplies. To some of his customers the Bible was quite unknown, and they carried it off as a hoarded treasure. Along with this there has been a decided slump in 'penny dreadfuls.' "

Oh, that such faith and fervor, such forsaking of sin, and such a Bible reading revival might come to America and other lands today! It will, if we will believe and "pray through."

CHAPTER VI

A PERSONAL VISIT
TO THE "FIRE-ZONE"

When the Welsh awakening began I was
in Liverpool, England, writing up the Torrey-Alexander revival meetings in that city
for various religious papers in America.

My soul was deeply stirred by the reports
of the revival in Wales. I longed to see the
spiritual awakening with my own eyes.

Accompanied by a friend I left Liverpool
to go to the center of the revival in Wales.
And here is the story of our visit, written just
after our return to Liverpool:

"I have just returned from a two days'
visit to the storm center of the great Welsh
revival which is sweeping over Wales like a
cyclone, lifting people into an ecstasy of spiritual fervor. Already over 34,000 converts
have been made, and the great awakening
shows no sign of waning. All observers agree
that the movement is fully as remarkable as
the memorable revival of 1859-60. It is sweeping over hundreds of hamlets and cities, emp-

tying saloons, theatres, and dance-halls, and filling the churches night after night with praying multitudes. The policemen are almost idle; in many cases the magistrates have few trials on hand; debts are being paid; and the character of entire communities is being transformed almost in a day. Wales is studded with coal mines, and it is a common occurrence to have prayer meetings held a thousand feet under ground amid the tinkle of the horses' bells and the weird twinkle of the miners' lamps.

"The leader of the revival is Mr. Evan Roberts, a young man only twenty-six years of age, who was a collier, and was later apprenticed to become a blacksmith. Then he felt a call to the ministry, and was a student in a preparatory school when the Spirit came upon him in such power that he felt impelled to return to his native village of Loughor and tell the people of God's love for them. He did so, and, as he spoke, the fire fell from heaven upon the community. The people were so stirred that they crowded into church after church, and remained until four o'clock in the morning. The flame spread from district to district throughout South Wales with almost incredible swiftness, and soon scores of towns

were being shaken by the power of God. From
the beginning, however, Mr. Roberts has been
the leader of the movement, and wherever he
goes the revival reaches fever heat. The fore-
most Welsh newspapers devote columns each
day to his meetings and give photographs of
him; and souvenir post-cards representing
him, are sold everywhere. Some idea of his
sudden fame may be gained from the fact that
sixty newspaper representatives endeavored
to interview him in two days recently.

"It was my good fortune to take two meals
with Mr. Roberts, and to attend three meetings he conducted. But let me give my impressions of the meetings and of Mr. Roberts in
order as they were formed during the visit.

"At noon on Tuesday I wired one of the
leading Welsh newspapers, asking where Mr.
Roberts would speak that evening. The reply
came back that he would be at Swansea for
the next two days. At 2 p.m. I left Liverpool
with an American friend, and we arrived at
Swansea at 9:30 p.m. Hastening to a hotel we
found it filled with visitors, who had come to
'catch the fire' of the revival. A second place
we found in a similar condition, but at the
third place we secured accommodations, and
then hastened to the church, which was for-

tunately situated in the down-town district. It
was 9:45 when we reached the place, and even
at that hour there were some scores of people
in the street seeking admission. But the gates
were closed and guarded by policemen, for the
church was already packed to the doors.

"Going up to one of the policemen I whis-
pered that I was an American journalist, and
that my friend and I were from Chicago.
These words acted like a magic charm, for he
at once asked us to come to another gate,
where we were speedily admitted and ushered
into the building. My first impression! How
am I to describe it? As we entered the door I
beheld a room, means to seat about 700 people, crowded to suffocation with about 1,500.
But this was not the chief thing that attracted
us. Up in the gallery a young lady was standing, praying with such fervor as I had rarely
if ever heard before. One hand was upraised,
and her tones were full of agonized pleading,
and though it was in Welsh, so that I could
not understand a word she uttered, yet it sent
a strange thrill through me. Then a young
man arose, and with rapt upraised face prayed
as though he were in the presence of the Al-
mighty. The entire atmosphere of the room
was white-hot with spiritual emotion, and my

chief thought was: 'This is a picture of what must have occurred in the early church in the first century of the Christian era.'

"A hymn was now started, and my attention was riveted on Evan Roberts, who stood in the pulpit and led the music with face irradiated with joy, smiles, and even laughter. What impressed me most was his utter naturalness, his entire absence of solemnity. He seemed just bubbling over with sheer happiness, just as jubilant as a young man at a baseball game. He did not preach; he simply talked between the prayers and songs and testimonies, and then rarely more than a few sentences at a time. Imagine a Christian Endeavor meeting where those present are wrought up to a pitch of holy enthusiasm until they are figuratively 'on fire,' and you will have a picture of the proceedings at Trinity Chapel that night.

"To my surprise the meeting terminated at 10:30. The reason for this, it was explained, is that Swansea is a city of nearly 100,000 population, and the people must go to their work early in the morning. We were also informed that Mr. Roberts was now usually ending the meetings at about this hour so as to avoid a nervous collapse.

"The next morning my friend and I went to the place where Mr. Roberts was staying, and were not only successful in securing a cordial interview, but were also invited to have luncheon with him. In appearance the young evangelist is of medium height, slender, brown-haired. He is extremely nervous in temperament, and his pallor showed the strain of the meetings upon him. When asked for a message for America, he grasped my hand, and gave me the following:—

" 'The prophecy of Joel is being fulfilled. There the Lord says, "I will pour out my Spirit upon all flesh." If that is so, all flesh must be prepared to receive. (1) The past must be clear; every sin confessed to God, any wrong to man must be put right. (2) Everything doubtful must be removed once for all out of our lives. (3) Obedience prompt and implicit to the Spirit of God. (4) Public confession of Christ. Christ said, "I, if I be lifted up will draw all men unto me." There it is. Christ is all in all.'

"The afternoon and evening meetings we attended were very largely like the first one, save that in each meeting the mood of Mr. Roberts was different. At the afternoon meeting, while describing the agony of Christ in the Garden of Gethsemane, he broke down and sobbed from the pulpit, while scores in the building wept with him. The meeting had been announced to begin at 2 p.m., but before 12 the building was packed, although it was at the edge of the city. It was with the utmost difficulty, aided by the police, that my friend and I squeezed ourselves in at the rear door, and then we stood near the pulpit scarcely able to move an arm. The air was stifling, but the people minded this not a whit. They had forgotten the things of earth, and stood in the presence of God. The meeting began about noon, and went on at white heat for two hours before Mr. Roberts arrived, and ended at 4:30 p.m.

"At the evening meeting Mr. Roberts was silent much of the time. For full twenty minutes he sat or stood motionless with closed eyes. But the meeting went on just as fervidly as though he were speaking. It was strange indeed to hear some one praying undisturbed while a hymn was being sung; or to hear two, three, or four engaged in prayer at the same time; yet, as has been so often remarked, there was perfect order in the midst of the seeming disorder. It was the Lord's doing, and it was marvelous in our eyes!

Made from an original drawing kindly lent by Fleming H. Revell, Jr.

DWIGHT L. MOODY
Moody moved two nations God-ward, when Heaven's fire
fell in his revival meetings in America and Great Britain.

REUBEN A. TORREY

Dr. Reuben A. Torrey, and his associate Charles M.
Alexander, were backed by the prayers of 20,000 people
banded together in prayer groups during their three years
of revival meetings in Great Britain.

"Presently a young girl—not over sixteen years of age—arose in the gallery, and began to pray. I understood not a word she said, but in a few seconds, in spite of myself, the tears were streaming down my cheeks. I looked up, and lo! old gray-haired ministers of the gospel were likewise weeping! There was something in the very tones of her voice that lifted one above the world, and pierced to the core of one's heart.

"It was nearly 10 p.m. when the most thrilling and beautiful incident of our visit occurred. A respectably dressed young man of about nineteen came down from the gallery, crying like a child, the tears streaming down his face as he staggered down the aisle towards the 'set fawr' (penitent form). He was nearly fainting when he got to the entrance to the big seat, and he threw his arms around the neck of the Rev. William James, the pastor of Ebenezer, which is the church he attends.

" 'Pray for me! Pray for me!' he shouted, as he embraced the minister who was moved to tears. The young man dropped into a chair. Mr. Roberts, who had been sitting on a chair in the pulpit, was on his feet. Something seemed to have told him what was the matter, and his face beamed with joy. Down the pulpit stairs he proceeded, and, on reaching the young man, threw his arms around him in a most affectionate manner. Mr. Roberts talked to him, and in a few minutes both were on their way to the pulpit. The young man was in first. What a change! The symptoms of being overcome had disappeared. His face had never worn a brighter appearance! 'Is mother here? Is mother here?' he shouted. A voice from the back of the chapel answered. 'Yes! Yes! She's here!'

"At this point every one in the audience was so deeply touched by the affecting scene that there was scarcely a dry eye to be observed. Some one started the Welsh hymn which is always sung when a person yields completely to God, and which has become the chant of victory of the revival. In thrilling and triumphant tones they sang fervently:—

> Diolch Iddo, diolch Iddo, diolch Iddo,
> Byth am gofio, llwch as llawr.

Which being interpreted means—

> Praises, praises, praises to God
> Who has remembered such as we are.

"When all was quiet, he said, 'Mother, I have had to give in! Yes, indeed! I tried to refuse, but I was compelled to submit!'

"A little later on he was calling for others to surrender, as it was 'grand.' He would not give his mother any more trouble! The mother broke into prayer, and when her son recognized her voice, he shouted, 'Well done, mom!' (Well done, mother.)

"Numerous accounts have been given of the beginning of the mighty awakening, no two of which agree. Some attribute it to a young girl who spoke at a Christian Endeavor meeting with such fervor that her hearers were melted into tears, and the flame started there. Others declare that it began when Evan Roberts went back to his native town of Loughor, two months ago, and set it on fire with his Spirit-filled pleading to accept Christ. But the fact is that the revival broke out in a score of places almost simultaneously, and Evan Roberts and the other young and fiery evangelists who have arisen during the last few weeks are largely the products rather than the causes of the awakening.

"The true origin of the movement is probably to be found in the prayer circles which have honeycombed Wales for the last eighteen months. The people who had banded themselves together were crying out mightily for

a revival, and God at length graciously answered the prayers of His saints. It is interesting to Americans to know how the prayer circles were started. A lady living in Australia
read a book by Dr. R. A. Torrey, in which
he reiterated the statement that we must 'pray
through' for revival. At that time Dr. Torrey
and Mr. Charles M. Alexander, noted American evangelists, were conducting their great
revival in Melbourne, the success of which
was largely due to the 2,000 prayer circles
which were held throughout the city. Shortly
afterward the lady, who had been so stirred
by Dr. Torrey's book, came to England.
She became the means of starting thousands
of prayer circles throughout the British Isles,
the object of which was to pray for a world-
wide revival. The answer to those prayers has
come in part in the Welsh awakening, and
may God speed the day when the revival fires
will spread all over Britain and America, and
throughout the entire world!"

CHAPTER VII

A MODERN PENTECOST

In the white-heat of the revival, Dr. G. Campbell Morgan, the well-known Bible teacher and expositor, made a special trip to Wales to get his own first-hand impressions of the awakening.

His soul was thrilled and his heart was filled with praise and thanksgiving to God for the things that he saw and heard. He returned to London and gave his congregation at Westminster Chapel a stirring account of his visit.

Dr. Morgan began by reading verses 15 to 18 of the second chapter of the Acts of the Apostles:

For these are not drunken, as ye suppose, seeing it is but the third hour of the day. But this is that which was spoken by the prophet Joel;
And it shall come to pass in the last days, saith God,
I will pour out of my Spirit upon all flesh:
And your sons and your daughters shall prophesy,
And your young men shall see visions,
And your old men shall dream dreams:
And on my servants and on my hand-maidens

I will pour out in those days of my Spirit; and they shall prophesy.

"I have not read these words as a text, but as an introduction to what I desire to say, as God shall help me, concerning the most recent manifestation of Pentecostal power. I refer to the great work of God that is going on in Wales at this time. In the simplest way I want to speak to you of what my own eyes have seen, my own ears heard, and my own heart felt.

"Yet I cannot help reverting, before going further, to the passage that I have read in your hearing. Peter stood in the midst of one of the most wonderful scenes that the world has ever beheld. When men said of the shouting multitudes that they were drunk, Peter said, No, these men 'are not drunken as ye suppose'; but 'this is that which was spoken by the prophet Joel.' If any one shall say to me, 'What do you think of the Welsh revival?' I say at once, 'This is that.'

"This is no mere piece of imagination, and it certainly is not a piece of exaggeration. 'I will pour out of my Spirit upon all flesh, and your sons and your daughters shall prophesy,' is the promise now evidently fulfilled in Wales. If you ask for proof of that assertion,

I point to the signs. 'Your young men shall
see visions!' That is exactly what is happening. It does not at all matter that this cynical
and dust-covered age laughs at the vision. The
young men are seeing it. 'And your old men
shall dream dreams,' and that is happening.
The vision goes forward, the dream goes back-
ward; and the old men are dreaming of '59,
and feeling its thrill again. Yea, 'and on my
servants and on my handmaidens, I will pour
out in those days of my Spirit, and they
shall prophesy.' It does not at all matter that
some regular people are objecting to the ir-
regular doings. 'This is that.' If you ask me
the meaning of the Welsh revival, I say, without one single moment's doubt, IT IS PENTECOST
CONTINUED.

"Let me talk familiarly and quietly, as
though sitting in my own room. I left London
on Monday, reaching Cardiff at 8:30 that evening, and my friend who met me said to me,
'What are you going to do? Will you go home,
or will you go to the meeting?' I said, 'What
meeting?' He said, 'There is a meeting in
Roath Road Chapel.' 'Oh,' I said, 'I would
rather have a meeting than home.' We went.
The meeting had been going on an hour and
a half when we got there, and we stayed for

two hours and a half, and went home, and the
meeting was still going on, and I had not
then touched what is spoken of as—it is not
my phrase, but it is expressive—the 'fire zone.'
I was on the outskirts of the work. It was a
wonderful night, utterly without order, characterized from first to last by the orderliness
of the Spirit of God.

"It was my holy privilege to come into the
center of this wonderful work and movement.
Arriving in the morning in the village, everything seemed quiet, and we wended our way
to the place where a group of chapels stood.
And everything was so quiet and orderly that
we had to ask where the meeting was. And a
lad, pointing to a chapel, said 'In there.' Not
a single person outside. Everything was quiet.
We made our way through the open door, and
just managed to get inside, and found the
chapel crowded from floor to ceiling with a
great mass of people. What was the occupa-
tion of the service? It is impossible for me to
tell you finally and fully. Suffice it to say that
throughout that service there was singing and
praying, and personal testimony, but no
preaching.

"It was a meeting characterized by a per-
petual series of interruptions and disorderli-

ness. It was a meeting characterized by a great continuity and an absolute order. You say, 'How do you reconcile these things?' I do not reconcile them. They are both there. I leave you to reconcile them. If you put a man into the midst of one of these meetings who knows nothing of the language of the Spirit, and nothing of the life of the Spirit, one of two things will happen to him. He will either pass out saying, 'These men are drunk,' or he himself will be swept up by the fire into the kingdom of God. If you put a man down who knows the language of the Spirit, he will be struck by this most peculiar thing. I am speaking with diffidence, for I have never seen anything like it in my life. While a man praying is disturbed by the breaking out of song, there is no sense of disorder, and the prayer merges into song, and back into testimony, and back again into song for hour after hour, without guidance. These are the three occupations— singing, prayer, testimony. Evan Roberts was not present. There was no human leader.

"As the meeting went on, a man rose in the gallery, and said, 'So and So,' naming some man, 'has decided for Christ,' and then in a moment the song began. They did not sing 'Songs of Praises,' they sang 'Diolch Iddo,' and the weirdness and beauty of it swept over the audience. It was a song of praise because that man was born again. There are no inquiry rooms, no penitent forms, but some worker announces, or an inquirer openly confesses Christ. The name is registered, and the song breaks out, and they go back to testimony and prayer.

"In the evening exactly the same thing. I personally stood for three solid hours wedged so that I could not lift my hands at all. That which impressed me most was the congregation. I looked along the gallery of the chapel on my right, and there were three women, and the rest were men packed solidly in. If you could but for once have seen the men, evidently colliers, with the seam that told of their work on their faces—clean and beautiful. Beautiful, did I say? Many of them lit with heaven's own light, radiant with the light that never was on sea nor land. Great rough, magnificent, poetic men by nature, but the nature had slumbered long.

"Today it is awakened, and I looked on many a face, and I knew that men did not see me, did not see Evan Roberts, but they saw the face of God and the eternities. I left that evening, after having been in the meeting three hours, at 10:30, and it swept on, packed as it was, until an early hour next morning, song and prayer and testimony and conversion and confession of sin by leading church members publicly, and the putting of it away, and all the while no human leader, no one indicating the next thing to do, no one checking the spontaneous movement.

"When these Welshmen sing, they sing the words like men who believe them. They abandon themselves to their singing. No choir, did I say? It was all choir. And hymns! I stood and listened in wonder and amazement as that congregation on that night sang hymn after hymn, long hymns, sung through without hymn-books. Oh, don't you see it? The Sunday-school is having its harvest now. The family altar is having its harvest now. The teaching of hymns and the Bible among those Welsh hills and valleys is having its harvest now. No advertising. The whole thing advertises itself. You tell me the press is advertising it. I tell you they did not begin advertising it until the thing caught fire and spread. And let me say to you, one of the most remarkable things is the attitude of the Welsh press. I come across instance after instance of men converted by reading the story of the revival

in the Western Mail and the South Wales
Daily News.

"Whence has it come? All over Wales—I
am giving you roughly the result of the ques-
tioning of fifty or more persons at random in
the week—a praying remnant has been agonizing before God about the state of the beloved
land, and it is through their prayers that the
answer of fire has come. You told me that the
revival originates with Roberts. I tell you that
Roberts is a product of the revival. You tell
me that it began in an Endeavor meeting
where a dear girl bore testimony. I tell you
that was part of the result of a revival breaking out everywhere. If you and I could stand
above Wales, looking at it, you would see fire
breaking out here, and there, and yonder, and
somewhere else, without any collusion or pre-
arrangement. It is a Divine visitation in which
God—let me say this reverently—in which
God is saying to us: See what I can do without the things you are depending on; see what
I can do in answer to a praying people; see
what I can do through the simplest, who are
ready to fall in line, and depend wholly and
absolutely on Me.

"What effect is this working producing
upon men? First of all, it is turning Chris-

tians everywhere into evangelists. There is
nothing more remarkable about it than that,
I think. People you never expected to see
doing this kind of thing are becoming definite
personal workers. Let me give you an illustra-
tion. A friend of mine went to one of the
meetings. He walked to the meeting with an
old friend of his, a deacon of the Congregational Church, a man whose piety no one
doubted, a man who for long years had
worked in the life of the church in some of
its departments, but a man who never would
think of speaking to men about their souls, although he would not have objected to someone
else doing it.

"As my friend walked down with the deacon, the deacon said to him, 'I have eighteen
young men in an athletic class of which I am
president. I hope some of them will be in the
meeting tonight.' Presently there was a new
manifestation. Within fifteen minutes the deacon left his seat by my friend and was seen
talking to a young man down in front of him.
Soon the deacon rose and said, 'Thank God
for So and So,' giving his name, 'he has given
his heart to Christ right here.' In a moment
or two he left him, and was with another
young man. Before that meeting closed that

deacon had led every one of those eighteen young men to Jesus Christ. And this was the man who never before thought of speaking to men about their souls.

"My own friend, with whom I stayed, who has always been reticent of speaking to men, told me how, sitting in his office, there surged upon him the great conviction that he ought to go and speak to another man with whom he had done business for long years. My friend suddenly put down his pen, and left his office, and went on 'Change,' and there he saw the very man he had come to seek. Going up to him, and passing the time of day, the man said to him, 'What do you think of this revival?' He looked his friend squarely in the eye and said, 'How is it with your own soul?'

"The man looked back at him, and said, 'Last night at twelve, for some unknown reason, I had to get out of bed and give myself to Jesus Christ, and I was hungering for some one to come and talk to me.' Here is a man turned into an evangelist by supernatural means. If this is emotional, then God send us more of it! Here is a cool, calculating business shipowner, that I have known all my life, leaving his office to go on 'Change,' and ask a man about his soul.

"The other day down in one of the mines—
and I hope you understand I am only repeat-
ing to you the instances that came under my
personal observation—the other day in one
of the mines, a collier was walking along, and
he came, to his great surprise, to where one
of the principal officials in the mine was standing. The official said, 'Jim, I have been waiting two hours here for you.' 'Have you, sir?'
said Jim. 'What do you want?' 'I want to be
saved, Jim.' The man said, 'Let us get right
down here,' and there in the mine, the mining
official, instructed by the miner, passed into
the kingdom of God. When he got up he said,
'Tell all the men, tell everybody you meet, I
am converted.' Straightway confession.

"The movement is characterized by the most
remarkable confession of sin, confessions that
must be costly. I heard some of them, men
rising who have been members of the church,
and officers of the church, confessing hidden
sin in their hearts, impurity committed and
condoned, and seeking prayer for its putting
away. The whole movement is marvelously
characterized by a confession of Jesus Christ,
testimony to His power, to His goodness, to
His beneficence, and testimony merging for-
evermore into outbursts of singing.

"Men are seeing God. Well, but you say that will pass. It is passing. The vision is passing out into virtue, and men are paying their debts, and abandoning the public-house, and treating their horses well. Did you say the next revival would be ethical? It is that, because it is spiritual, and you will never get an ethical revival except in this way. Vision is merging into virtue. Theatrical companies are packing up and going back because there are no audiences, and on every hand there is sweeping down these Welsh valleys a great clean river. It is the river of God, and men are being cleansed in it, in personal and civic relationships. Tradesmen are being startled by men paying debts. An emotion that will make a man do that is worth cultivating, and it is good all the way through.

"No man ever yet could describe a burning bush, and I know I have not described this to you.

"There is nothing so important as the saving of men, and when the church says that, and is ready, God will come. We need then to wait upon Him in earnest, constant prayer. Oh, brothers, sisters, pray, pray alone! pray in secret! pray together!"

CHAPTER VIII

WHEN THE FIRE FELL
IN RECENT YEARS

In a glorious manner the divine fire fell from heaven in connection with the remarkable meetings conducted by Dwight L. Moody and Ira D. Sankey in Great Britain and America. The great evangelistic campaigns of these Spirit-filled evangelists stirred England and America more deeply than any similar meetings since the days of Wesley and Whitefield in England, and of Charles G. Finney in the United States.

Mr. Moody was a clerk in a shoe store in Boston, Mass. He was converted and mightily filled with the Holy Spirit. Mr. Sankey was a master of gospel song. When they joined forces, and were backed by multitudes of praying people, they moved two great nations Godward.

When Moody and Sankey visited the British Isles, they filled the largest buildings to overflowing. Multitudes of all classes were saved, and great multitudes of Christian people were

set on fire for God. Many years after the close
of their meetings in Great Britain, I was informed that great numbers of the earnest
Christian workers in the various churches in the
British Isles were the outcome of the Moody
and Sankey meetings. In America the evangelists kept revival fires burning in multitudes
of hearts and homes and churches for many
years as they went up and down the land holding revival meetings that taxed to capacity
great halls in many large cities. One of the en-
during monuments of Moody in America is
the Moody Bible Institute in Chicago which
has trained many thousands of Christian
workers for valiant service for God, both in
America and in foreign lands.

Moody himself gratefully acknowledged
that it was the prayers of an invalid woman
that caused the fire to fall from on high at the
beginning of their revival meetings in the
British Isles!

It was nothing less than a great volume of
intercessory prayer that sent Dr. R. A. Torrey
and Mr. Charles M. Alexander sweeping
around the world like a gale from heaven. It
is estimated that 100,000 souls professed faith
in Christ during their world-wide revival tour.
Their meetings in Melbourne, Australia, were

preceded by 1700 cottage prayer meetings! No
wonder the fire fell from heaven and the great
Melbourne Exhibition Building was crowded
with eager listeners and multitudes were saved.
For three years Torrey and Alexander held
meetings in Great Britain and again the cities
were shaken by the power of God as in the
days of Moody and Sankey. It was my privilege to be with Torrey and Alexander during
their last nine months in Great Britain. Once
more great buildings were filled to overflowing,
and the famous "Glory Song" swept over the
British Empire more rapidly, it was said, than
had ever been done before by any song sacred
or secular. Messenger boys whistled it as they
went about the streets on their errands; pianos
rang it out in the homes and on trans-Atlantic
liners. The very atmosphere of heaven was in
the revival meetings.

And what was the secret of it all? Dr.
Torrey told me that during their three years
of meetings in the British Isles 20,000 people
were banded together in Prayer Groups all
over the land praying for their meetings, and
that this was in addition to the intensive prayer
in each city where they held their revival meetings. It was prayer—earnest, continuous, persistent, believing intercession—that was the

secret and the source of the power in their great meetings!

Once more the fire fell from heaven in connection with the round-the-world revival meetings of Dr. J. Wilbur Chapman and Mr. Charles M. Alexander. They also held great meetings in Australia, Great Britain and America, with multitudes saved, and multitudes of Christians wondrously quickened in the faith. It was my privilege to be a member of the Chapman-Alexander party as they visited these and other lands.

The Chapman-Alexander meetings in Boston, Massachusetts, deeply stirred that famous New England city. The newspapers carried big headlines about the progress of the work. Newspaper reporters were carrying New Testaments in their pockets. Multitudes of people were born again into the kingdom of God.

From Boston the evangelists sailed for Australia from Vancouver, Canada. As they journeyed across the continent holding meetings en route, many thousands of intercessors were enlisted. Then in Australia multitudes more of prayer partners were added. What was the result? The Chapman-Alexander meetings in Sydney, Melbourne, Adelaide, Brisbane, and other places were not simply another series of evangelistic meetings. As the people of America and Australia mingled their petitions before the Throne of Grace the fire once more fell from heaven and wondrously moved the Australian Commonwealth God-ward.

Here is just one example of the untold blessing that followed. The soul of a pastor in Adelaide, Rev. Lionel Fletcher, was so stirred by the power of God in the meetings that he himself became a flaming evangelist. He went throughout the British Empire in the power of the Holy Spirit and saw tens of thousands of young people confess Christ and dedicate their lives to His service.

Again and again it has ever been the same story of fire falling from heaven in answer to prayer. Intercessory prayer was the secret of blessing in the Chapman-Alexander meetings! It was the secret in the Torrey-Alexander campaigns! And it will ever be the open secret of revival blessing! God still hears and answers the earnest, continued cry of His children!

Who can estimate the untold blessing of the Billy Sunday revival meetings throughout the length and breadth of the United States? Praise God for the hundreds of thousands who professed faith in Christ in his meetings. Praise God for the towns and cities that were moved

God-ward by his meetings as the fire fell from heaven.

And what was the secret of Billy Sunday's power with God and men? Again it was intercessory prayer. Billy would not go to a town or city until they had formed and held cottage prayer meetings. Sometimes the revival began even before Mr. Sunday arrived in the city.

Recently I was talking with a minister who was the pastor of a church in Trenton, New Jersey, when Billy Sunday had his city-wide campaign there. The pastor told me that as the result of the Billy Sunday meetings he took 170 people into his church, and that they were the backbone of that church today.

"And what shall I more say" of the great meetings of Gypsy Smith and many other Spirit-filled evangelists who have gone up and down this and other lands borne on the wings of intercessory prayer, and seeing multitudes saved, and multitudes quickened in the faith?

And praise God for the Youth for Christ movement, and the Saturday night meetings that are spreading so rapidly in this and other lands. More power to the arms of all those who are conducting these youth meetings! This movement is one of the most hopeful harbingers of revival on the spiritual horizon today.

Oh friends, God still hears and answers the earnest, persistent, fervent intercession of His children, and opens the windows of heaven today just as truly as in days gone by!

Let us keep on praying, both individually and in prayer groups, until another great spiritual awakening sweeps over our land, and even to the uttermost parts of the earth!

There are three ways in which each one who reads these lines can have a real and vital share in helping to bring about national and world-wide revival:

1st. You can pray earnestly for revival each day in your own home. Send for a prayer card for your own use day by day, and for a supply to give to others to enlist their prayers for revival.

2nd. Form, if at all possible, a prayer group to pray daily or weekly for revival in this land and throughout the world. A man in Manila in the Philippine Islands recently read this book and has started a prayer group which meets daily to intercede for revival.

3rd. If you can possibly manage it, please lend this book to ten other persons, and urge each one who reads it to purchase his or her own copy, and lend it in turn to 10 people. In this way an ever-increasing volume of prayer will be enlisted for national and world-wide revival.

* * * * *

Dear Reader: Will you not take the message of this book to your own heart? Please ask the Lord to empower *you* for intercessory prayer for revival and to help you to enlist others to become intercessors. In this way *you* can have a very real and vital share in helping to bring glorious spiritual awakening to this and other lands!

"And I sought for a man among them, that should make up the hedge, and stand in the gap before me for the land, that I should not destroy it: but I found none." Ezekiel 22:30.

God forbid that we should fail to stand in the gap for our beloved land!

How You Can Further Revival
in America and Other Lands

Please lend this book to 10 people, and urge them to pray earnestly for revival.

We hope that everyone reading a borrowed copy of "When the Fire Fell" will order his or her own copy and lend it to 10 friends. In this way, by the grace of God, an ever-increasing circle of prayer for revival among ourselves and all nations will extend throughout the world.

Please use the lower part of this slip to order your copy of the book. *The Lord will surely reward you for your help in promoting revival.*

(Suggested form for ordering books)

MILLION TESTAMENTS CAMPAIGNS,
1505 Race Street, Philadelphia 2, Pa.

Dear Sirs:
Enclosed find $................for which please send me................copies (copy) of "When the Fire Fell." I wish to help in promoting revival by distributing this book.

Name..

Street & Number..

City & State..

Order one or more copies as the Lord leads. Price: 1 copy, 25 cents. Quantity prices *to one address:* 5 copies, $1.00; 12 copies, $2.00; 25 copies, $4.00; 50 copies, $7.75; 100 copies, $15.00.

My Prayer Covenant

With God's help I will endeavor to have a special time of prayer each day for revival in our land and throughout the world.

TEN PRAYER SUGGESTIONS

1. Heavenly Father, I thank Thee for the great revivals of the past that have led multitudes of souls into the glorious light of the gospel.

2. Forgive, I beseech Thee, my sins and the sins of our nation. Pour out Thy Spirit upon us and bring us back to Thee. Send revival to my own heart and to the hearts of great multitudes.

3. Raise up speedily, I beseech Thee, multitudes of individual intercessors, and great numbers of prayer groups, to intercede earnestly for revival in this land and throughout the world.

4. Send revival, I pray Thee, to our own church. Pour out Thy Spirit upon our pastor, and upon the officers and members of the congregation.

5. Send revival among those who are still in our armed forces at home and abroad. Fill the chaplains with Thy Spirit, and make them soul-winners.

6. May our President and his associates, be truly born-again men. May

See other side for 6 to 10.

BOOK-MARK PRAYER CARDS SENT FREE

Send for a supply of these attractive book-mark prayer cards, printed in two colors, to give to praying people in your church and community. A small gift to help defray the cost of the cards will be appreciated.

BACK OF PRAYER CARD

they be given wisdom from on high to combat the evils in our nation, and to rule in righteousness and justice.

7. I thank Thee for giving us victory in the world war. But now, I beseech Thee, deliver us from communism, modernism, drunkenness, and other evils from within, that would destroy our beloved land.

8. May the pure gospel be kept on the air in spite of all opposition; and may increasing multitudes, in this and other lands, be born again through this God-given radio ministry.

9. May more missionaries than ever before be sent forth by Thee during the coming years, to preach the gospel in the power of the Holy Spirit.

10. May funds be provided, and great numbers of these prayer cards be distributed; and may those who use them pray in faith for revival day by day.

All these things I ask in the Name of our Lord Jesus Christ, Amen.

*   *   *   *

Send for a supply of these cards to give to praying people. They will be sent free of cost, but it will be appreciated if something can be forwarded to help pay the cost of the printing and distribution of the cards.

PRAYER FOR REVIVAL
Room 1302, 1505 Race Street
Philadelphia 2, Pa.

Send for only as many cards as you feel you can use to good advantage in your church and community. Do not let the cards lie on the shelf. Place them quickly in the hands of intercessors to help in bringing another great spiritual awakening to our nation in this hour of crisis.

BLESSINGS FOR TEN PEOPLE—AND MORE!

This book is the property of

NAME..

ADDRESS...

We suggest that the owner of this book lend it to at least ten friends, to multiply the revival blessings, and to help in increasing intercession for revival and victory.

Please give a copy of the "My Prayer Covenant" card to each one who reads the book. If you do not have a supply of these cards, please send for them. They will be forwarded free of cost as the Lord provides.

When this book is lent to you, please read it as soon as possible, and return it to the owner, noting date received and date returned.

Names of Readers	When received	When returned
1. Name....................................	....	....
2. Name....................................	....	....
3. Name....................................	....	....
4. Name....................................	....	....
5. Name....................................	....	....
6. Name....................................	....	....
7. Name....................................	....	....
8. Name....................................	....	....
9. Name....................................	....	....
10. Name....................................	....	....